PUPPIES
AMAZING PUPPY FUN FACTS AND TRIVIA FOR KIDS

Learn How to Raise a Puppy to Become a Loving Dog (WITH 40+ PHOTOS!)

Medical Disclaimer: The ideas and suggestions contained in this book are not intended as a substitute for consulting with your veterinary physician. All matters regarding your puppy's health require medical supervision.

Legal Disclaimer: all photos used in this book are licensed for commercial use or in the public domain.

Table of Contents

INTRODUCTION

Aren't puppies just the cutest thing *ever*?

I mean, how can your heart not melt when you look at this beautiful **tiny ball of fluffiness**??

Don't you just want to take him home, right NOW?

If you're the type of person that stops walking each time you spot a puppy, **you've come to the right place**.

This book is full of **fun puppy facts** and **trivia** that will:

- warm your heart
- make you smile, *and*
- teach you a little something about what it takes to raise a puppy with love and care.

Moreover, this book contains lots of **beautiful color photos** of the <u>**cutest puppies**</u> **you've ever seen**!

And at the end, there's a '**Puppy Quiz**' with 23 questions to test your newly gained puppy knowledge.

Here are some of the questions you will be able to answer at the end of this book:

- Why do puppies look so cute?
- What is the origin of the word 'puppy'?

- What is the name of the first dog in space?
- Which dog breeds do not have pink tongues?

I hope that sparked your curiosity...

Whether you already have a puppy, or simply want to learn more about these wonderful little beings: *this* is the book for you!

So, let's dive straight in, shall we?

101 PUPPY FACTS

1.

A puppy is born blind, deaf, and toothless. The eyes of a puppy are closed when they are born, and it takes about 1–2 weeks before they open. Touch is the first sense a puppy experiences. So be very gentle when you pick them up!

2.

In the U.S. alone, more than 5 million puppies are born every year.

3.

When a puppy is first born, it spends 90% of its life sleeping. And the other 10%? Eating! Not a bad life, huh? In these first weeks, they need a lot of rest so their body can develop and grow. After a few weeks, their sleep hours reduce to around 14 hours per day. This is actually quite similar to a human newborn.

4.

When puppies have become fully grown dogs, they need less sleep. On average, a dog sleeps about 10 hours per day.

5.

Like human babies, Chihuahuas are born with a soft spot in their skull. This is called the molera, and it closes up as the puppy grows.

6.

In the English language, the word 'puppy' exclusively refers to dogs, whereas the word 'pup' is used for other mammals, such as giraffes or seals.

7.

Depending on the breed, some puppies can weigh 1-3 lb, while larger puppies can weigh up to 15-23 lb.

8.

When is a puppy no longer a puppy? A puppy is considered an adult when it reaches the age of one. At what age your puppy reaches maturity depends on its size and breed.

Generally speaking, the smaller the breed, the sooner the puppy reaches maturity. For example, a Chihuahua puppy is considered a full-grown dog at about 10 months old. A German shepherd, however, takes about 15 months to fully mature.

9.

When a puppy turns one year old, it is as physically mature as a 15-year-old human being.

10.

It takes 4 weeks for a puppy to fully develop the ability to hear.

11.

And it takes even longer, 6 weeks on average, until they develop full vision. Once a puppy's senses have fully developed, it can – finally! – start exploring the world in earnest.

12.

Because their senses are still developing, for the first six weeks, puppies will want to stay very close to their mother. Around that time, the mother will start teaching what it means to be a dog, by encouraging them to be a bit more independent and venture out of the nest.

Keep this in mind when considering getting a puppy: As a rule of thumb, it would be best to let the puppies stay with the mother and the rest of the litter for 8–10 weeks.

13.

Speaking of getting a puppy: how do you choose the right puppy to take home? If you don't have a lot of experience with dogs, it would be best to go 'middle of the road.'

Don't take the puppy that, as tiny as he is, is bullying his brothers and sisters. He might be a handful when you take him home. On the other hand, a puppy who isolates himself from the litter by staying in a corner might be difficult to socialize.

14.

Looking at a mixed breed puppy, and not sure
how big he's going to be? Then take a look at
his paws! If, when looking at them, you wonder:
hmmm, will he ever grow into his feet? Then
there is a good chance you'll end up with a
medium to large sized dog!

15.

Most human babies tend to cry a lot. Puppies, however, don't cry as much as adult dogs. Why is that? Because the eyes of a puppy aren't very moist when they are born. As they grow older, their eyes get wetter. When a puppy is about 10 weeks old, the level of tears is the same as that of an adult dog.

16.

A woman carries her baby for 9 months. A female dog only carries its puppies between 58 and 68 days, roughly 9 weeks.

17.

If puppies are born by cesarean and cleaned up before given back to the mother, there is a risk that the puppies are rejected by her.

18.

Puppies are born toothless. When they are 6–8 weeks of age, they will have developed a full set of 28 baby teeth. Shortly after, the puppy's permanent teeth will begin pushing out the milk teeth. When they are about 7 months old, a puppy will have 42 permanent teeth.

19.

Have you ever seen that YouTube video of a sleeping dog, laying on its side and moving his legs quickly as if it were running? All dogs dream! However, puppies tend to dream more frequently than adult dogs.

20.

At the end of the song "A Day in the Life", The Beatles recorded a high-pitched whistle that only dogs can hear! Paul McCartney did this specially for his pup, Martha.

21.

Although socialization continues throughout a dog's life, between 3 and 14 weeks of age is a critical socialization period. This is a period of rapid brain development.

It is important that puppies recognize and interact with dogs, humans and cats early on, as early as 3 weeks old. At this age, they are old enough to be aware of and able to respond to their environment.

22.

Ever heard of the term 'puppy love'? The earliest known use of this phrase for a brief romantic attachment between young people was in 1823.

23.

Puppies are born in litters of just 2 to as many as 16.

24.

In 2004, a Neapolitan mastiff gave birth to 24 puppies. This is the largest litter ever recorded.

25.

After about 15 days, puppies can stand up. And when they are 21 days old, they are usually able to walk.

26.

Did you know the word puppy is centuries old? It dates back as far as the 15th century. The word puppy evolved from the Middle French word 'poupée', which can be translated as 'doll' or 'toy'.

Eventually, the meaning of the word puppy changed from 'toy dog' to 'young dog'. Around this time, the word 'puppy' replaced the word 'whelp'. As a verb, 'whelp' is still used. For example: 'Whelping a litter of puppies'.

27.

When naming your puppy, keep it short. Your puppy only listens to the first syllable of a word! If you name him 'Captain Johnson III', the only part he will recognize is 'Cap'!

28.

Another reason to keep your puppy's name short is that it helps when teaching him to follow short commands, like 'sit'. Longer syllable words, especially a name that he will hear over and over again, can be confusing.

29.

The Peanuts book 'Happiness Is A Warm Puppy' by Charles Schultz was first published in 1962.

30.

Ever wondered why puppies are so cute? The answer: baby schema.

Say what?!

Baby schema are certain features that most baby mammals have in common, like: big eyes, large heads, and soft textures.

These features make them appear cute. Human babies also have these traits. This means that when you see a puppy, your brain recognizes the features that would make you relate to your own baby, which causes a release of the feel-good neurotransmitter dopamine.

31.

Puppies have a strong urge to chew. If you care about your sofa, make sure you have enough doggie toys laying around!

32.

80% of dog owners buy their dog a present for birthdays and holidays.

33.

And more than 50% of dog owners sign holiday cards from themselves and their pets!

34.

At around 75 million, the United States has the highest pet dog population in the world. Who's in second place? France.

35.

Puppies can sense your feelings.

36.

In 2007, researchers found that a puppy can understand your gestures, such as pointing. They tested puppies that were 6, 8, 16 and 24 weeks old.

And although they found that all puppies could understand the human cue, they also observed that those skills improved over time. So, the older the pup was, the better he was able to understand the cue.

37.

According to a 2011 study, the average purebred dog litter consists of 5.4 puppies. How many puppies a dog whelps varies per breed though.

Older and smaller dogs tend to have fewer pups. Where on average Rhodesian Ridgebacks give birth to 8.9 puppies at a time, Poodles and Pomeranians only give birth to 2.4 puppies per litter.

38.

'Puppy water', which is simply puppy pee, was once highly regarded as a cosmetic. Mary Doggett's 'Book of Receipts', published in 1684, contained a recipe for 'puppy water'. Supposedly, it is good for removing wrinkles and improving the quality of the skin.

39.

Each day in the U.S., 15 dogs are born to each human born. With these birth rates, many pups will never find a home. Therefore, it is important to spay or neuter your pup.

40.

You've probably heard about the amazing reproductive potential of rabbits. However, did you know that your puppy can have her own puppies? According to some sources, one unspayed female dog, her mate and their puppies can produce up to 67,000 puppies in six years!

41.

Most pups can be spayed or neutered when they are between 6 and 9 months old.

42.

In 1957, Laika, a Russian stray, was the first living mammal to orbit the Earth, in the Soviet Sputnik spacecraft. Unfortunately, she died in space. However, there is a silver lining to the story: Laika had a daughter, Pushinka, who later had four puppies with President John F. Kennedy's terrier, Charlie.

43.

Ever wondered why your toddler and your pup get along so well? Because your dog is as smart as a 2-year-old toddler. A puppy understands roughly the same words and gestures, up to 250!

44.

Depending on the breed, a puppy reaches its full size between 12 and 24 months.

45.

Although they are born deaf, dogs quickly surpass our hearing abilities. Not only can dogs hear 4 times as far as humans. They can also hear a wider frequency range than humans. Whereas a human can hear high pitched sounds up to 23,000 Hertz, a dog's frequency range goes up to 45000 Hertz.

46.

As with humans, a dog's hearing decreases with age.

47.

The American Kennel Club, or AKC, was founded in 1884. It is the most influential dog club in the United States.

48.

According to the AKC, when a puppy is about 6 to 12 weeks old, they need to eat four small portions of food a day to meet nutritional demands. It is important to monitor your pups and teach them proper portion control.

49.

Puppies double their weight in a week.

50.

Puppies need some time to get used to their body, because it grows pretty fast. Similar to a toddler learning to walk, a puppy can be a bit clumsy when it learns to walk. They will stumble and fall. It can take some puppies up to five weeks to figure out how to walk properly.

51.

When they are between 3 – 4 months old, puppies begin to lose their baby teeth. They are replaced by their adult teeth.

52.

Puppies are vulnerable to illnesses. They are most vulnerable to parvo and distemper when they are 4 to 12 weeks old. Newborn puppies are also vulnerable to the canine herpesvirus in their first weeks. They can contract it from their mother or other dogs in the household.

53.

It is very important that a newborn puppy is not
separated from his mother and littermates for
the first 8 weeks. If you take them away earlier,
their immune system is not fully developed yet,
which leaves them more vulnerable to infectious
diseases.

54.

Once you adopt a puppy, they need to be vaccinated and dewormed. Take them to the vet when they are around 8 weeks old. Around this time, puppies should also receive their first vaccinations.

55.

Davy Crockett, a 19th-century American folk hero and politician and popularly known as 'King of the Wild Frontier', once said: *"I would rather be beaten and be a man than to be elected and be a little puppy dog."*

56.

47% of U.S. households own at least one dog.

57.

According to Rover's (the largest network of pet sitters and dog walkers in the U.S.) 2017 annual dog names report, the most popular male dog names are Max, Charlie and Cooper. The most popular female dog names? Bella, Lucy and Daisy.

58.

The largest dog breed is the Irish Wolfhound. The largest dog ever recorded was Zeus, a Great Dane, who measured a whopping 44 inches tall in 2011!

59.

The smallest dog breed is the Chihuahua. According to the Guinness Book of World Records, the smallest living dog is a Chihuahua named Milly. She was born on 1 December 2011, and is only 3.8 inches high.

60.

Dogs have been around for many years. The earliest dog fossil dates all the way back to 12,000 B.C.

61.

According to the AKC, the 5 most popular dog breeds are: Labrador Retriever, German Shepherd, Golden Retriever, Bulldog and Beagle.

62.

In their first 4 – 5 months, puppies grow to half their body weight. Then, it takes about a year or more to gain the remaining half of their adult body weight.

63.

Larger dog breeds mature slower than smaller ones.

64.

A dog's nose is so powerful that they can smell it if someone is sick. According to scientific research, dogs can discover lung cancer by sniffing a person's breath. And some dogs' noses are so well developed that they can even detect cancer that is still too small to be detected by a doctor! So, make sure you pay attention when a dog acts funny around you.

65.

Petting a puppy lowers your blood pressure.

66.

The first modern guide dogs were trained to help soldiers who had lost their sight due to exposure to mustard gas in WWI.

67.

'Buddy', a female German shepherd, was the first guide dog in America. He was trained by Dorothy Eustis, an American dog breeder living in Switzerland.

After reading an article she wrote, Frank Morris, a blind man from Nashville, asked her to train a guide dog for him. When Morris returned to the U.S. with Buddy, they went on a publicity tour to raise awareness for the needs of blind people, and the abilities of guide dogs.

68.

In 1929, Frank Morris and Dorothy Eustis co-founded 'The Seeing Eye.' This was the first guide dog school for the blind in the U.S., and it still operates today.

69.

What makes a puppy a good guide dog candidate?

Parents, particularly the mother, are a good indicator of how the puppies will turn out as adults. Additionally, studies done in the 1950s showed that if a puppy does well in a retrieving exercise, there is a high chance that it will also successfully complete guide dog training school.

70.

What's a dog's favorite kind of pizza?

Pupperoni!

71.

Just like every human has a unique fingerprint, every dog has a unique nose print. One problem though: because their noses are always wet, taking nose prints will be really hard!

72.

All dog breeds have pink tongues, with two exceptions: Chow Chow and Shar Pei. Their tongues are black. Chow Chow puppies are born with pink tongues. However, after about 8-10 weeks, their tongues turn black.

73.

Are you allowing your puppy to pee on a lamp post? This could be more dangerous than you think! Dog's urine contains corrosive acids, which can corrode metal. In Croatia, some lamp posts actually collapsed because so many dogs were peeing on them!

74.

Puppies love affection. However, they can also feel jealous when their owner displays affection towards someone or something else.

75.

In 1992, the American artist Jeff Koons, known for his large-scale reproductions of everyday objects, created the artwork 'Puppy' as a monument to the sentimental: a 43-foot-tall sculpture of a West Highland Terrier made with stainless steel, soil, and carpeted in bedding plants. It can be seen outside of the Guggenheim Museum in Bilbao, Spain.

76.

Puppies can't regulate their own body temperature very well. To ensure their immune system and other bodily processes function properly, it is important that they are kept in a setting of approximately 75 degrees Fahrenheit.

77.

Josh Hutcherson, who played Peeta in 'The Hunger Games' film series, adopted a Pit Bull puppy that had been at the Downey Animal shelter for 110 days.

The puppy arrived at the shelter with a broken leg and two missing toes.

However, he was able to get surgery before Hutcherson took him home.

He named him Driver, after Ryan Gosling's character in the 2011 movie Drive.

78.

Newborn puppies rely on their mothers to stimulate them to go to the bathroom. They can't eliminate waste on their own.

If the puppy's mom isn't around, you can help your puppy by gently rubbing its rear end with a wet paper towel until they defecate and urinate.

79.

Puppies are born with sharp little nails. It's best to wait with clipping their nails until they are 4 – 6 weeks old, unless their sharp nails are hurting the mother.

80.

If you have kids, it is best to choose a kid-friendly dog breed when adopting a puppy. Dog breeds like Labrador or Golden Retrievers, Collies and German Shepherds are highly trainable. Therefore, they are more kid-friendly than some other dog breeds.

81.

If you pick up a puppy, make sure you place one hand under their rump and the other supporting the chest, with the puppy's arms and paws hanging over the second hand.

82.

Want to give your puppy a bath? You can begin bathing your puppy when it's 8 weeks old.

Start small: begin with the kitchen sink, before you put them in a big bathtub. Fill the kitchen sink with just a few inches of lukewarm water and place the puppy in it.

This allows your puppy to get used to being bathed, in a safe environment.

83.

Puppies are high on energy and are still discovering the world around them. When your pup takes off with something that you do not want them to have, your first impulse may be to chase them. Try this instead: turn the situation into a game, where *you* run away and make the puppy chase *you*. And watch how easy it is to retrieve the item!

84.

When you adopt a puppy, and take him home
for the first time, take him out for a walk
immediately. Your new roommate is likely going
to be both stressed and excited from the car
ride and the new environment. This will trigger
him to urinate or defecate, and you don't want
him to wet your kitchen floor on the first day.

85.

If your puppy pees or poops outside, during a walk, give him a compliment, or even a little treat. If you wait until you get home, he won't make the connection; he may think the treat is for walking through the door!

86.

If you find your puppy peeing inside, immediately say "Hey!", or clap your hands loudly, and rush him outside. While you want to be firm, never scold your puppy when this happens! He may become afraid to pee in front of you, which can cause all kinds of problems in the future.

87.

If you're too late, use a clean sponge to sop up the floor, and put any wet tissue paper or poop in a bag. Don't use bleach. Instead, use a product like Odor-Out, which is available at Walmart.

When you're done, don't throw the bag away yet! Instead, take it outside to a place where your puppy is allowed to pee, and wipe the tissue paper on the ground. Then, let your puppy sniff it. This will make him understand that, next time, this is where he needs to do his business.

88.

Puppies are happier and feel more secure if they are given a doggie bed. This is a place where they can retreat in case they feel stressed. Make sure to place it in a quiet part of the house.

89.

In 2012, Jennifer Aniston adopted a black and white Pitbull puppy. Aniston had a hard time picking just one puppy from the litter. In an interview, she said: *"We were there for three hours, and I'm telling you, I was almost walking out with three puppies. It's so hard. That's why we named her Sophie, because it was Sophie's Choice. I was crying – it was so hard"*.

Sophie's Choice is the title of a 1979 novel by William Styron. The novel is about a Polish woman in a Nazi concentration camp. She has two children. She is forced to make the impossible decision which of her two children will live and which will die.

90.

Some puppies may cry for up to a week when they first move into their new home. They miss their mother and littermates. Allow your puppy this grieving time (it will pass!), and – respecting its boundaries – give it a lot of affection.

91.

Almost all puppies go through a phase where their baby fur falls out and is replaced by their adult coat. For most dog breeds, this happens gradually and you may not even notice it, aside from some shedding.

However, Pomeranians are the exception to this rule, and there's even a name for the phase they go through: 'Puppy Uglies'. They lose practically all their fur in a short amount of time, and will remain that way for a couple of months before their adult fur appears.

92.

Every dog sheds. Through this process, the body rids itself of old, unhealthy hairs and replaces it with new, healthy hairs. Being a canine, fur is very important for your puppy in order to keep warm and stay protected from the elements. Therefore, make sure you routinely brush your puppy, removing the old fur.

93.

If you have to leave your house and your puppy home alone (especially the first few times), experiment with putting on the television or radio. This way, they can hear some noises, which may prevent them from being overcome by loneliness and feeling abandoned.

94.

A good rule of thumb is: *A [X] month old puppy can hold their bathroom needs for [X] hours.* So, a 3-month-old puppy can hold their bathroom needs for 3 hours, et cetera.

This rule of thumb is true until they are 8 months old. Make sure you take your puppy out multiple times a day, so it can do its business.

As a bonus, you will keep your kitchen and living room floors clean and odorless!

95.

If your puppy shows signs of aggression to another person, correct them gently, but firmly. Never pick them up! Your puppy may interpret this as a reward for its (unwanted) behavior.

96.

Some dogs bark a lot. The best way to prevent this from happening is teaching your puppy that barking doesn't equal you showing up 5 seconds later.

If you hear your puppy barking in the middle of the night, and you know he doesn't need to go to the bathroom, ignore it.

If you show up every single time they bark, they will learn that they can get your attention by barking. Even at 3am...

97.

A cool trick you can use to teach your puppy not to bite is to say "Ouch!" loudly when he bites or nips you. You can even pretend that it really hurt. In a litter, a puppy yelps loudly if it gets bitten by another puppy. So, by imitating this, your puppy understands that he shouldn't be doing this.

98.

Dogs are social animals. They enjoy being part of a pack with people. This is even more important for a puppy. So, keep your puppy close. Dogs that spend too much time outside, on their own, can develop anxiety, aggression, and other mental health issues.

99.

Just like humans, dogs need proper dental care in order to prevent gum disease and cavities. Therefore, it is best to get your puppy used to having his teeth brushed early on.

Try brushing his teeth at least a few times a week, daily would be even better. You can use a small, soft toothbrush, with toothpaste for dogs. Also take your dog to the vet for a dental check-up every other year.

100.

If you have a puppy *and* a cat, keep their food separated. Cat food is very unhealthy for dogs. It is not properly balanced for them in terms of nutrients, and the amount of protein can be hard on their liver and kidneys.

101.

A 2017 study by the University of Lyon at Saint-Etienne found that puppies respond stronger to so-called 'baby talk', where human adults raise the pitch of their voice, than to normal voices.

The effect fades over time though; adult dogs don't care, and respond to both types of voices in the same way.

PUPPY QUIZ

1. Can puppies see when they are born?

2. What is the first sense puppies experience?

3. How many puppies are born in the U.S. every year?

4. What percentage of time does a newborn puppy sleep?

5. Puppies from which dog breed are born with a soft spot in their skull?

6. When is a puppy no longer considered a puppy?

7. How long does it take for a puppy to fully develop its ability to hear?

8. How long does a female dog carry its puppies before giving birth?

9. Are puppies born with teeth?

10. Which song by The Beatles contains a high-pitched whistle that only dogs can hear?

11. In 2004, a Neapolitan mastiff gave birth to the biggest litter ever recorded. How many puppies did she give birth to?

12. What is the origin of the word 'puppy'?

13. How many syllables of a word does a puppy listen to?

14. Why do puppies look so cute?

15. The U.S. has the highest pet dog population in the world. How many dogs are kept as a pet in the U.S.?

16. What is 'Puppy Water'?

17. What is the name of the first dog in space?

18. Fill in the blank: Dogs can hear … times as far as humans

19. What are the most popular dog names for male and female dogs?

20. According to the Guinness Book of Records, what are the largest and smallest dog ever recorded?

21. What is the most popular dog breed, according to the American Kennel Club?

22. What was the name of the first guide dog in the U.S.?

23. Which dog breeds do not have pink tongues?

PUPPY QUIZ ANSWERS

1. No, puppies are born blind. The eyes of a puppy are closed when they are born, and it takes about 1–2 weeks before they open. It takes another 3 weeks for them to fully develop their vision.

2. Touch. So be very gentle when you pick them up!

3. More than 5 million.

4. 90%. When puppies have become fully grown dogs, they need less sleep. On average, a dog sleeps about 10 hours per day.

5. Chihuahuas.

6. A puppy is considered an adult when it reaches the age of one. At what age your puppy reaches maturity depends on its size and breed. Generally speaking, the smaller the breed, the sooner the puppy reaches maturity.

7. 4 weeks.

8. 9 weeks.

9. No, they are born toothless. After 6–8 weeks, puppies have 28 baby teeth. These are later replaced by 42 permanent teeth.
10. 'A Day In The Life'. Paul McCartney included this whistle for his pup, Martha.

11. 24.

12. The word 'puppy' evolved from the Middle French word 'poupée', which can be translated as 'doll' or 'toy'. Eventually, the meaning of the word puppy changed from 'toy dog' to 'young dog'. Around this time, the word 'puppy' replaced the word 'whelp'. As a verb, 'whelp' is still used. For example: 'Whelping a litter of puppies'.

13. Only 1. So, keep it short when naming your dog!

14. Because they have certain features, called 'baby schema', that most baby mammals have in common: big eyes, large heads, and soft textures. These features make them appear cute. Human babies also have these traits.

15. Around 75 million.

16. 'Puppy Water' is nothing more than puppy pee. Centuries ago, it was highly regarded as a cosmetic. It was believed to help remove wrinkles and improve the quality of the skin.

17. Laika. In 1957, Laika, a Russian stray, was the first living mammal to orbit the Earth, in the Soviet Sputnik spacecraft.

18. 4.

19. Male: Max, Charlie and Cooper.
Female: Bella, Lucy and Daisy.

20. Largest: Zeus, a Great Dane, 44 inches.
Shortest: Milly, a Chihuahua, 3.8 inches.

21. Labrador Retriever.

22. Buddy, a female German shepherd. She was the dog of Frank Morris. He later co-founded 'The Seeing Eye' in 1929, the first guide dog school for the blind in the U.S.

23. Chow Chow and Shar Pei. Their tongues are black.

FINAL THOUGHTS

Have you ever watched South Park? If so, you may know that many episodes end with a conversation between Stan and Kyle that starts with: *"You know, I think I've learned something today."*

Well, I hope *you* have also learned something today. And had a lot of fun in the process!

You already knew that puppies are cute.

But now you also have a better understanding of what it is like to *be* a puppy.

And, if you are lucky enough to raise a puppy of your own, you now also better understand how you can connect with your puppy, and how to make sure it develops into a well-behaved dog.

Raising a puppy changes your life. I really hope you get to experience this for yourself!

Let's end of a light note: *What do you call a frozen dog?*

A pupsicle!

Thank you again for reading this book, and I wish you (and your puppy) all the best!

OTHER BOOKS BY THE AUTHOR

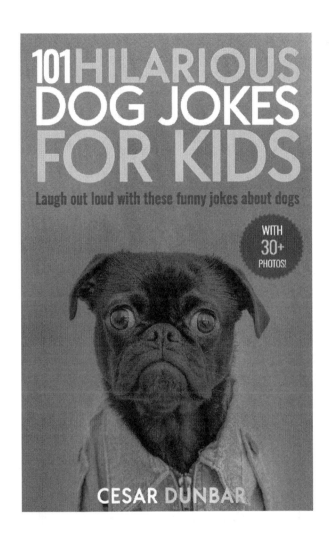

PUPPY
TRAINING 101
THE ESSENTIAL GUIDE TO
RAISING A PUPPY WITH LOVE

Train Your Puppy and Raise the Perfect Dog Through Potty Training,
Housebreaking, Crate Training and Dog Obedience

CESAR DUNBAR

DOG
TRAINING 101
THE ESSENTIAL GUIDE TO RAISING A HAPPY DOG WITH LOVE

Train The Perfect Dog Through House Training,
Basic Commands, Crate Training and Dog Obedience.

CESAR DUNBAR

BONUS CHAPTER: HOW DOES A PUPPY THINK?

*This is a bonus chapter from my book **'Puppy Training 101**: The Essential Guide to Raising a Puppy With Love.' Enjoy!*

***

"There is no psychiatrist in the world like a puppy licking your face."

Bernard Williams

Ever wondered what your dog is thinking about? Read on to find out more.

Would you like to know what your dog might be thinking?

Wouldn't that be wonderful? Perhaps you have thought of a situation where your dog is able to clearly communicate with you. Unfortunately, this is nothing more than wishful thinking.

However, you can develop a basic understanding of the psychology of your puppy.

***

Staring

"What are you thinking?" you might wonder, as your puppy is looking at you longingly. If you have already fed him and have also taken him out for a walk, it might be really difficult to figure out what he is thinking. Dogs tend to gaze at their owners, intently. Probably this isn't a sign of boredom.

He is probably staring at you intently because he wants a treat, wants to play, or just wants you to pet him for a while. Your dog might also be doing this because he wants some extra attention and love.

***

Looking Sad

Do you feel really guilty when you leave your puppy home alone and head out to work the whole day? You might worry that your dog would be sad the whole day. Unless your puppy has separation anxiety, your puppy will be perfectly fine. In fact, if you have a dog walker checking in on your dog, then the puppy would greet him with a wagging tail. Your puppy might seem confused or even sad when you leave, but they tend to get used to your routine. They tend to adapt themselves to it. However, it is really important that your dog knows the difference between your usual work schedule and a long trip.

***

Barking Repeatedly

Does your puppy tend to keep barking whole night long? It might seem like the only reason he's doing this is to keep you from getting any sleep. You will need to remember that they bark for a particular reason. Your puppy isn't barking to annoy you. Your puppy might be doing this to get your attention.

A dog usually barks when it wants something. Perhaps a treat, to go on a walk, or even to be freed from its confinement. It could also be because your puppy senses danger and he wants to let you know. Or he is excited and wants to play with you. Dogs tend to learn by repeating their behaviors. If your puppy has discovered that by barking, he gets something that he wants, he will keep on doing it.

***

Cocking Their Head

You might have noticed that your dog tends to tilt his head to the side when you speak to him. This is definitely not because your puppy understands the story you are telling him. They tend to cock their head for multiple reasons. Your puppy might be hoping to better understand a word you are saying, or something that sounds familiar. Your puppy might also be cocking his head so that he can hear you better. Or perhaps to get a better look at your face to understand what you are saying.

Attempting to understand what goes on within your puppy's mind is an ongoing practice. After a while, you will be able to understand what your dog wants by just one look of theirs.

***

This is the end of this bonus chapter.

Want to continue reading?

Then go to the Amazon website and search for "puppy training 101"

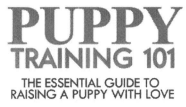

Train Your Puppy and Raise the Perfect Dog Through Potty Training, Housebreaking, Crate Training and Dog Obedience

CESAR DUNBAR

Hope to see you there!

Made in the USA
Lexington, KY
20 March 2019